THE LOUGHBOROUGH ROAD CAR
COMPANY LIMITED

A history of the first bus service
in the Loughborough district

By John Bennett

Cover picture caption: Spring 1914 - the crew of Loughborough Road Car Company's new Daimler double-decker pose proudly with the vehicle at the Bull Ring, Shepshed. (S. Evans)

ISBN No. 1 872863 06 X

Published by Kithead Limited,
De Salis Drive, Hampton Lovett, Droitwich Spa, Worcs, WR9 0QE

Contents

SKETCH PLAN
OF
LOUGHBOROUGH & DISTRICT LIGHT RAILWAYS
—— 1900 ——

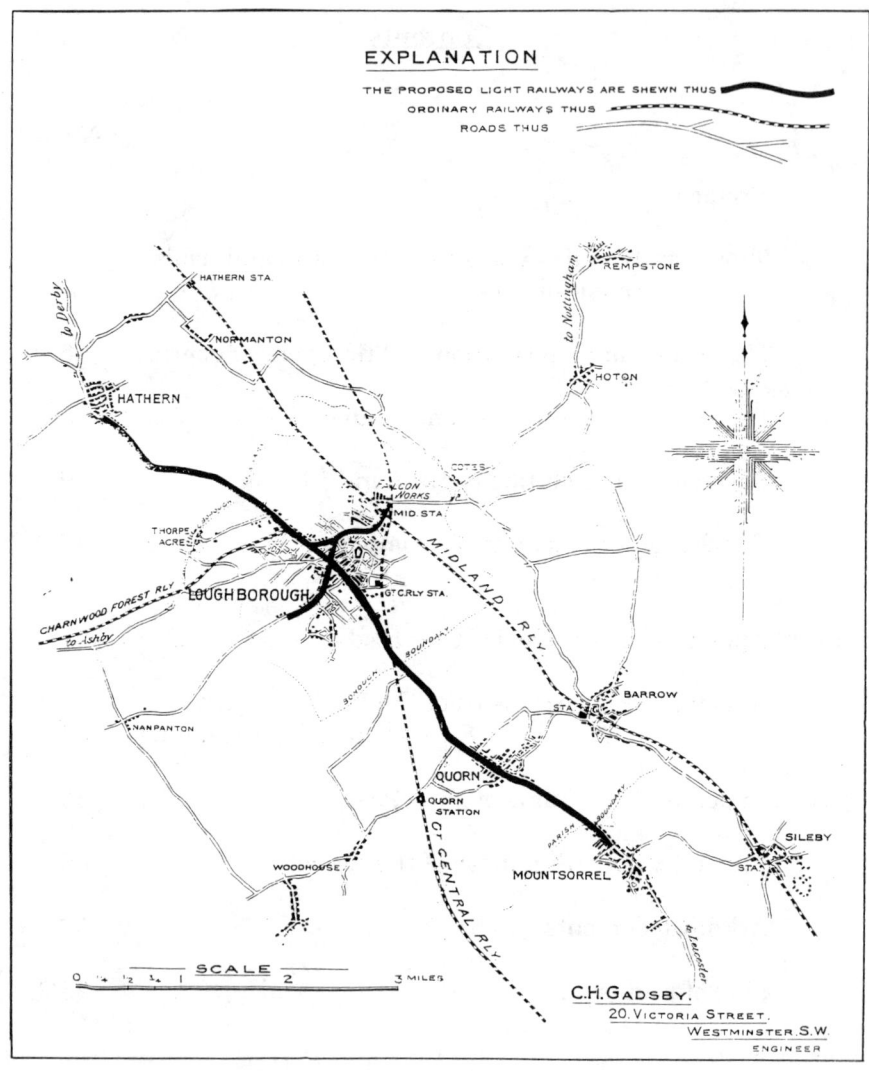

The tramway proposals of 1900, from the original prospectus once in Loughborough Public Library.

4

PREFACE

Those who are familiar with modern Loughborough, a thriving market town with important engineering and pharmaceutical industries and a notable University of Technology, must revise their perceptions of the place dramatically to appreciate the period discussed in this book.

In the early years of this century, Loughborough was still being forced to accept its new dependence upon factories with almost one-tenth of the population of 21,000 being employed by the Brush Electrical Engineering Company. A number of local gentlemen had sought to ensure the future of the town by creating the Borough (1888), providing supplies of water (1870 and 1907), gas (1899) and electricity (1903) as well as arranging for the disposal of sewage (1895).

Leaving the Market Place by any of the main roads, open country was reached in little over half a mile. The edge of the town at the time is still indicated to a great extent by the change from terraced housing to the semi-detached properties of the 1930's, although there were a number of large detached residences on the fringes. Loughborough has expanded in every direction of the compass but development to the east has been restricted by the flood plain of the River Soar. The present Shelthorpe and Dishley housing areas were all agricultural land and Thorpe Acre was a small village outside the town.

The roads themselves would be unrecognized today, thick with mud in the winter and dry and dusty in the summer. The standard treatment was to harrow the surface, add stones, which were obtained from the quarry at Nanpantan and broken up by men from the Workhouse, and then to roll the whole lot flat. In the town the prepared surface was additionally sprayed with tar! The present roads have not only a superior surface, but often take different routes, hence New Ashby Road (A512) has replaced Old Ashby Road, the

Leicester road (A6) no longer has any appreciable dip at "Bull in the Hollow" and the Derby road (also A6) is very much straighter than it was in years past.

The inspiration for writing the history of the Loughborough Road Car Company came from the realization that those who, for many years, had claimed that nothing was known about the company were mistaken. Motor vehicles were a novelty and made news, so the local weekly newspapers, the *Loughborough Monitor & News*, *Loughborough Herald and North Leicestershire Gazette* (founded 1880) and the *Loughborough Echo* (founded 1891) reported many of the company's activities in detail, as well as regularly carrying advertisements and timetables. The Minute Books of the various council committees, essentially those of the Sanitary Committee, whose responsibilities encompassed anything that impinged on public health, and that included buses, were an invaluable source of information. Official files from Companies House, now lodged at the Public Record Office at Kew gave precise details of everything from finance to shareholders. There are few people alive today who remember the company, although my interview with 91 year old William Stothard was a real education, but there are many present day inhabitants of Loughborough whose forebears were connected with the Road Car and stories do get passed down. The interpretation of what became a bulging file of information is entirely my own.

John P. Bennett
November 1993

TRAMS AND TRIALS

The town of Loughborough grew rapidly in the last thirty years of the nineteenth century, developing from a small market town on the turnpike road between London and the North-West into an important hosiery and engineering centre. Borough status was achieved in 1888 and the new council quickly set about attracting new industries and making major improvements to amenities.

Herbert Morris Limited opened their Empress Works in 1897 to build a whole range of lifting gear and cranes whilst in 1889 the Brush Electrical Engineering Company had taken over the existing Falcon Works established by Henry Hughes in 1865. Steam tram-engines and railway locomotives were built but in 1895 a major expansion of the works was initiated to enable up to 750 tramcars a year to be produced. Much of the production went to the associated British Electric Traction Company Limited (BET) which was developing tramway systems in towns all across the country, although many municipal systems also operated Brush tramcars. In the early years of the twentieth century, Brush also built cars, lorries and buses powered by petrol engines but this activity had ceased by 1907, probably due to considerable financial difficulties as a result of a damaging strike which lasted over six months in the previous year.

With over one thousand of the town's workforce employed there, it is hardly surprising that Brush promoted a tramway scheme for the town. A company was formed, entitled "The Loughborough and District Electric Traction Syndicate Limited". An application was made to the Board of Trade in November 1899 for a Light Railway Order under the terms of the Light Railway Act of 1896, with the first directors of the new company being named as Robert Percy Sellon, Bertrand Broadhurst and Robert Dawbarn, none of whom were local men. Powers were sought for nine railways, totalling 8.25 miles, to provide two routes, one from Hathern in the north to Mountsorrel in the south and a second between the Falcon Works and Forest Road. Crucial to this second route was the opening up of a new street between the Market Place and Toothill Road to provide the east side of triangle of track in the town centre. This development which would have cleared some notoriously poor quality property, required a contribution of £10,000 from Loughborough Corporation. The narrow main thoroughfares of High Street and Swan Street could not be used for through running of the trams due to their width, thus the services to Hathern and to Mountsorrel would have had to operate separately.

Enclosed electric tramcars, built to a gauge of three feet six inches, were to be operated, usually as single vehicles, but with trailer cars available at busy periods. Electricity would be supplied through overhead wiring, the support posts of which were available to the Corporation to provide street lighting, and the new company sought to generate electricity as the the town had no supply at this time. The service frequency provided on the Forest Road route would be every few minutes, with cars every fifteen to thirty minutes to Hathern and Mountsorrel. It is interesting to speculate whether the increased trade, property values and housing development promised, would have occurred.

The engineer for the scheme. Mr C.H. Gadsby, estimated the cost of construction to be £74,613 and the company was authorized to raise capital of £120,000. The local authority was to have the right to purchase the system after 27 years and every 7 years thereafter at a fair market value.

A Public Enquiry opened at the Police Court in Loughborough on 19th March 1900 and resumed again on 2nd April when the Earl of Jersey and Colonel Baughey viewed the routes, agreeing to all except that to Hathern. After an Inquiry at the Board of Trade in London on 2nd May 1901, powers were granted for 6.5 miles of tramway and the order was confirmed on 21st December 1901. The "Loughborough and District Light Railway Company" was incorporated by the Light Railway Order to operate the system.

The Town Council were very much in favour of the scheme, the County Council very much against, but it was the adverse financial market of the time which prevented construction as the necessary capital was not forthcoming and when the powers lapsed four years later the scheme was lost for ever. In retrospect it seems unlikely that the company would have been successful as there was insufficient population to generate the necessary passenger traffic.

At a meeting of the Tradesmen's Association in February 1905 it was resolved to ask the Council to provide a motor-bus service for the district, especially on market days, to improve trade in the town. In the surrounding villages that did boast a railway station it was in every case located well away from the village proper and at Loughborough itself the three stations were each a good distance from the Market Place. The Council was interested in the concept of a bus service but had no powers to operate one themselves, although they readily agreed to a trial run in a vehicle of the Electric Vehicle Co. Ltd in July 1908. The thirty-four seat double-deck bus arrived from York on Tuesday 14th July, was charged at the Electricity Works during the night and demonstrated in the Market Place on Wednesday afternoon. A run out via Nanpantan to the Blackbrook Reservoir (completed in 1906) was undertaken, returning by way of Ashby Road, a severe hill climbing test for any vehicle, but apparently achieved silently and smoothly at a steady 14 miles per hour. In October of the same year the Council agreed to grant the company licences to operate six vehicles but no more was heard of the scheme.

Just over a year later, in November 1909, the Council members sampled another bus, during a few hours stop on a journey from Blackpool to London. The vehicle had been in Blackpool for Aviation Week when its owner challenged aviators to fly within a quarter mile of its powerful eighteen inch marine electric searchlight, thus testing the theory that the light was as effective a deterrent as a battery of quick firing guns! The bus itself was a Hallford-Stevens petrol-electric machine of rather handsome proportions.

William A. Stevens of Maidstone, whose company manufactured dynamos and electric motors, had successfully converted a car to operate on the petrol-electric principle and then continued development work which culminated in the entry into service of a petrol-electric bus in January 1908 in the London fleet of Thomas Tilling Limited. The patents were held by the S.B.& S. Syndicate, the gentlemen concerned being Percy Frost Smith, Frank Brown and William A. Stevens. The chassis was built by J. & E. Hall Ltd of Dartford, who were noted for the excellence of their vehicles at the time, and had a 30hp four-cylinder petrol engine. In the petrol-electric system, the engine drove a generator which supplied current to the electric motors, the final drive being by means of shafts and gears to the rear wheels. The benefits of the system were the smooth and simple control of the vehicle.

The Council was suitably impressed but a local newspaper which reported the trial asked laconically "when will we have these or any other buses?". A possible answer actually came quite quickly, for at the Council meeting on 6th December 1909 a letter was read from Mr W.A. Stevens in which he sought the approval and support of the Council in forming a small company to operate buses between Loughborough, Barrow, Cotes, Hathern, Mountsorrel, Nanpantan, Normanton, Quorn, Shepshed and Zouch. Once it was established that the support would be moral not financial, a resolution approving the suggestion was agreed to. Developments were slow and it was not until June 1910 that a special meeting of the Tradesmen's Association was held to consider the motor-bus proposal. It was necessary to raise £3,300 capital and a number of local gentlemen agreed to meet the preliminary expenses. A further meeting of all interested parties was held at the Town Hall on 24th June 1910 to approve the scheme. King Edward VII died on 6th May 1910 and as a mark of respect all newspaper columns for this period were separated with thick black lines.

Finally in September 1910, well over five years after the first discussions, the motor-bus arrived. Registered D 4782, it was a Hallford-Stevens petrol-electric vehicle, almost a year old, and fitted with a twenty-two seat rear-entrance bus body of a rather Parisian appearance. The main compartment held fourteen passengers, the smoking compartment a further six, all on longitudinal seats, and two more could ride alongside the driver. On Monday 19th September, Mr Stevens addressed a party of guests, after entertaining them to lunch at the Bulls Head Hotel, and outlined the events leading up to the inauguration of the three months trial service between Shepshed, Loughborough and Mountsorrel. The speech indicates that a second visit was made by a vehicle shortly after that of November 1909 and that both were at the invitation of Mr W.H. Allen, the Borough Electrical Engineer. Mr Allen was appointed to this post in November 1904, having previously been the assistant, and his guiding hand is quite clearly behind all the motor-bus developments.

Unfortunately the bus sank into the soft ground of the hotel yard, some reports say into an old cess pit, and so it was not until Tuesday morning that the first trip was made, to Mountsorrel, carrying a party of local gentlemen. A photographer recorded the occasion and the bus entered service with a journey at twelve noon to Shepshed. The event was well reported locally and both *Motor Traction* and *Commercial Motor* the leading national trade magazines of the day, carried a report and photograph, such was the novelty of the service. The timetable was arranged so that the bus operated at 8 a.m. and on each even hour until 8 p.m. to Shepshed and at 9 a.m. and each odd hour until 9 p.m. to Quorn and Mountsorrel. The journey time on both routes was twenty-five minutes, allowing a five minute wait before each departure. A late service on Saturday at 10 p.m. to Shepshed was also offered; on the first Saturday of operation three bus loads of would-be passengers awaited this departure - the ladies travelled, the men walked! The fare was 4d for each journey, with 1d stages; a parcels delivery facility was also provided. In the first four and a half days 2608 passengers were carried and demand often exceeded capacity. Argus, a columnist in a local newspaper reported the progress of the trial in detail but, whilst he approved of the enterprise, he felt that it was "just sufficient to upset the people to whet their appetite, and then they would have to wait until next summer" for a full service; in fact they waited much longer.

In the second week 2179 passengers were carried and for the third week a service to Woodhouse Eaves was added leaving Loughborough at 1.10 p.m. and 6.50 p.m.. The extra mileage destroyed the even headway service and considerably reduced the total number of journeys so the original timetable was restored a fortnight later with the addition of an 11 p.m. Saturday journey to Quorn. The murder of Mrs Crippen and her husband's conviction in October, the town fair in November and a General Election on 9th December deflected newspaper interest away from the buses but it was reported that on 5th January 1911 Mr Stevens met seven of the main supporters at the Bulls Head to review the experiment. During eleven weeks ending on 2nd December 1910, the bus ran 7,470 miles, with £221 in receipts and expenditure at 8d. a mile. The meeting adjourned with a resolution to form a local company with prominent local gentlemen as directors. It is of interest that the Council's Sanitary Committee recommended one omnibus licence be granted to W.A. Stevens Ltd of Maidstone and omnibus drivers' licences to

C.M. Agutter of Maidstone and W.H. Allen of Loughborough at its meeting on 21st September 1910; by the time this received Council approval the trial was almost halfway through!

In spite of the apparent success of the service and the fact that over £800 of the estimated capital needed to form a company had been promised, very little was heard about buses for another twelve months, whilst the villagers no doubt returned to the trains, horse-drawn waggonettes or their own legs for transport to town. However, in March 1912 Mr Allen had two very long letters published in the *Loughborough Echo* and the idea of a bus service was rekindled. Referring to the 1910 trial, Mr Allen observed that a service with temporary garage, staff and vehicle, operating fourteen hours a day, six days a week, was bound to suffer breakdowns, although these had been few and it had really been bad weather and the state of the roads which had terminated the trial. Since that time several meetings had failed to get sufficient support to form a company, especially since Directors, each with a minimum £25 shareholding, had not been forthcoming. However, perhaps it had been a good thing not to proceed sooner as the vehicles now available were much improved. He now envisaged a company with a capital of only £2,000 operating two buses with electric lighting, hot water heating, removable side windows for summer use, seating 28 passengers and capable of 14 m.p.h. whilst returning 8 miles per gallon fuel consumption. A garage was available, the same route and fares as the trial service could be used with the addition of routes to Woodhouse Eaves and Nanpantan. A bicycle on top of each bus would enable the driver to cycle for help in the event of a breakdown! It could not be left to the Corporation to institute the service as this would require an Act of Parliament.

Mr Allen had certainly done his homework and a week later the same newspaper carried an equally long letter which outlined the various possible transport systems, electric trams, trolley vehicles and motor vehicles powered by battery, steam or petrol. As an electrical engineer Mr Allen favoured the petrol-electrics which he had driven and ridden on in the service of Thomas Tilling in London; the vehicles were available at about £800 each.

This certainly sparked off discussions in the town, although the next meeting of the Tradesmen's Association on 18th March 1912 was rather more concerned about the proposal to change the day of the weekly market which was, and still is, held on a Thursday. Mr Allen spoke at the meeting and had evidently consulted with the committee in advance; his proposal was adopted and £850 promised by 29 of those present.   Delivery of the buses was promised in four months if ordered immediately.   All tradespeople were to be circulated and a number of letters of support appeared in the local press, including one from Mr T.W. Bailey, President of the Tradesmen's Association.   It finally looked as if Loughborough was to get its buses and, as if to prove it, the *Loughborough Echo* of 29th March 1912 carried a photograph of one of Tilling's double-deckers.

THE LOUGHBOROUGH ROAD CAR CO.

PUBLIC APOLOGIES.

I THE undersigned George Cotton, of Forest-road, Shepshed, hereby apologize to the Loughborough Road Car Co. Ltd., for my behaviour in the 'bus which proceeded from Loughborough to Shepshed at 7 p.m. on Saturday, the 21st inst. I undertake not to repeat such conduct in the future.
(Signed) GEORGE COTTON.
March 26th, 1914.

I THE undersigned Horace Wilfred Miller, of Queen-street, Shepshed, hereby apologize to the Loughborough Road Car Co. Ltd., for my behaviour in the 'bus which proceeded from Loughborough to Shepshed at 11 p.m. on Saturday, the 21st inst. I undertake not to repeat such conduct in the future.
(Signed) HORACE WILFRED MILLER.
March 26th, 1914.

The Company hereby give notice that they intend to put a stop to disorderly conduct in their 'buses. A set of Bye-laws and Regulations have been framed and submitted to H.M. Board of Trade for confirmation. These will duly be published and summary proceedings will be taken in any subsequent cases of disorderly behaviour.

Public Notice in the *Loughborough Echo* of 27th March 1914

DUPLICATE FOR THE FILE.

No. 121652

Certificate of Incorporation

I Hereby Certify, That the

Loughborough Road Car Company, Limited

is this day Incorporated under the Companies (Consolidation) Act, 1908, and that the Company is **Limited**.

Given under my hand at London this *Twenty-sixth* day of *April* One Thousand Nine Hundred and *twelve.*

Fees and Deed Stamps £ *7 · 0 · 0*

Stamp Duty on Capital £ *12 · 10 · 0*

Geo. Marqual

Registrar of Joint Stock Companies.

Certificate received by *H.H.Johnston*

for Solicitors Law-Stationery Society

28/9 Chancery Lane W.C.

Date *29th April 1912*

The Companies Registration Office copy of the Road Car Company's Certificate of Incorporation.

14

NEW COMPANY

Mr Richard Sutton Clifford (Junior) of Messrs Clifford & Clifford, solicitors, was appointed to make the legal arrangements involved in creating and registering a new limited company and on 24th April 1912 he was able to call the directors together to sign the relevant documents. The gentlemen concerned were Messrs W.F. Charles, W.H. Allen, A.E. Armstrong, H. Clemerson, J. Deakin, A.J. Pilsbury and H.F. Young, all of whom were closely involved with businesses in the town. The forms were quickly despatched to Companies House in London and on 26th April the Certificate of Incorporation was granted, followed on 9th May by a further certificate entitling the company to commence business. The Loughborough Road Car Company Limited (company number 121652) was legally ready to trade.

A considerable number of documents had to be prepared and their survival gives a great deal of information about the early days of the company. The Chairman was Mr W.F. Charles, the Secretary Mr F.G. Fleeman and the auditors Messrs Herbert Godkin and Co., whilst the registered office was at 1 Frederick Street, the home of Mr W.H. Allen. The company was authorized to issue 9,000 £1 shares, with a minimum allotment of £1,500 to enable it to proceed. A return made to Companies House in June shows that £2197 worth of shares had been issued between 7th May and 31st May and by the end of July 2500 shares were allotted, all for cash.

153 individuals or companies held shares, the vast majority local people, from all walks of life, many only investing £5, others up to £100. The major shareholders included Messrs W.F. Charles, W.B. Paget, A.B. Proudman, F.R. Griggs, H. Morris and F. Beck. The last named was a retired coal merchant from whom the garage premises were purchased, whilst the others were prominent local businessmen and gentlemen who could be relied upon to support any venture in the public interest. A large number of shopkeepers, publicans and lodging house keepers also subscribed. Almost every

trade was represented - framework knitter, grocer, engineer, surveyor, clothier, athletic outfitter and tobacconist, hosier, plumber, monumental mason, wine merchant and many more, some of whose businesses survive today, Boots Cash Chemists (Eastern) Ltd and W.S. Hepworth (Ladybird Books) for example.

The Articles of Association for the new company were some seventeen pages long, containing thirty-eight clauses covering every aspect of operation and conduct. Essentially the company stated that it was "to carry on business as motor car, omnibus, van and cab proprietors and carriers of passengers and goods". Many headings refer to standard clauses in the 1908 Companies Act but it is interesting to note that the company could operate in any part of the world whilst the directors, who had complete indemnity in the event of financial failure, could be disqualified from office by virtue of bankruptcy, lunacy or absence from meetings for more than six months without leave.

A meeting was held at the Town Hall on 2nd August 1912 to receive and consider the Statutory Report of the formation. Subscriptions for shares now amounted to £2314 of which £420 had been deposited against the order for the bus chassis, £100 on the purchase of the garage and £55 of an estimated £70 spent on legal expenses, leaving a balance of £1700 at the bank. The garage, latterly a coal merchant's premises, but previously the Assembly Rooms, occupied a site of 620 square yards of which just over forty feet fronted on to the thoroughfare known as The Rushes. The company acquired it in July 1912 from Mr Frederick Beck for £500, of which £100 was to be taken in shares, and the remainder being raised by means of a mortgage on the property, the deal being concluded by Mr Allen.

At the meeting of the Council's Sanitary Committee on 19th June it was recommended that the company be granted two omnibus licences and a licence to store petroleum at the garage, 400 gallons, in fifty gallon barrels, to be kept in a pit. Licences for storing petrol, and calcium carbide which was used to make acetylene gas for lighting, were required to be renewed annually.

It might seem that everything was progressing well, but this was far from the truth. Everything was ready but of the buses, the most essential equipment, there was no sign.   Mr S.T. Topping, printer (and shareholder) raised the issue with Mr Allen at a Tradesmen's Association meeting on 25th October, three months after it had been anticipated that the buses would commence operation.   A letter in the local press a month later reported that over forty chassis were being bodied at the Brush works, thirty for one company, and the writer concluded wryly that the "Road Car is being fooled or is fooling us".

The full answer was not revealed until the first Annual General Meeting, held at the Town Hall on Monday 30th December, by which time the chassis had finally arrived and were at the Brush works for the fitting of the bodies.   Only a few people were present at the meeting but they learned that the chassis were ordered on 11th May for delivery on 27th July.   The makers, blaming a dock strike for the delay, promised delivery by the end of August but letters to the firm on 14th, 21st, 31st August and 7th September produced no result, in spite of the last dated letter threatening to effect a penalty clause.   Action was taken on 18th October and an arbitrator was appointed by the Institute of Engineers, resulting in a promise of delivery by 18th November, failing which a penalty payment of £126 and also £55 costs would be made by the makers.   The company received the payment on 23rd November but it was almost a month later before the local press could announce that the chassis were ready.   Mr Allen spent the weekend of 21st and 22nd December at Maidstone testing the chassis and drove north on Sunday evening, arriving without mishap in the small hours of Monday morning at Loughborough.

It is difficult to know where the fault lay, although it was probably in over-optimistic promises of delivery, but after some considerable wooing of the town by Mr Stevens in 1909 and 1910 the company suddenly wanted two chassis in May 1912, by which time Mr Stevens had developed new buses and new markets and he can hardly be criticised for that.   In October 1910 it was reported in the *Commercial Motor* that due to the increasing demand for J. & E. Hall Limited's gear driven chassis, all petrol-electric vehicle construction would move to W.A. Stevens Ltd's Maidstone works and so the link with Halls was severed.

The latest Stevens petrol-electric vehicles, as they were now known, were much more sophisticated machines with a single electric motor between the chassis members directly coupled to a Dennis rear axle. Examples were stated to be in service at The Hague and in central India! Thomas Tilling Ltd financed further development during 1911 and by June a new model was ready for testing. This became known as the Tilling-Stevens TTA1 model and it featured a 30 h.p. four-cylinder petrol engine, with the radiator behind it and a Renault pattern, or "coal scuttle" type bonnet. The engine drove a generator and motor, placed below the driver, and a propellor shaft and worm-driven back axle provided the final drive. The pressed steel chassis had a wheelbase of 13 ft 6 ins, an overall length of 19 ft 4 ins and weighed three tons, seven hundredweight. After a failed attempt to acquire premises at Hadley in Shropshire, it was decided in November 1911 to expand at Maidstone, which involved building a new factory.

Over 140 chassis were on order for Thomas Tilling, four for Newcastle Corporation and 40 for the Birmingham & Midland Motor Omnibus Co. Ltd (Midland Red) in Birmingham, this latter operator requiring quick delivery beginning in May 1912, just when the Loughborough order was received and whilst the new factory was still under construction. At the end of November 1912, Mr Stevens demonstrated a new version of the chassis in London prior to a luncheon at the Holborn Restaurant. The radiator was moved to the traditional position at the extreme front of chassis behind which was a 40hp engine and more powerful electrical equipment to cope with the hills on the Harborne route in Birmingham. The vehicle demonstrated was for Liverpool Corporation, to whom it was delivered in early December and it was two examples of this new model, designated TTA2, that were finally delivered to Loughborough in the same month.

The Brush works constructed the bodies, reputedly in July 1912, to a very high standard. The frame, of ash pillars, was panelled in mahogany and featured four windows on each side of the saloon; the upper portion of each window dropped down and each was provided with a curtain. The seats had ash frames with oak laths; twenty-nine passengers could be accommodated, all facing forward. A sliding door led on to an open platform where the driver was seated, without any protection from the elements, the same man doubling as

The Hallford-Stevens omnibus D4782 in High Street, Loughborough on the trial route to Mountsorrel in 1910.   Alongside the driver is W.H. Allen.   (D. Bean collection)

The sponsors of the trial service pose for a photograph at Mountsorrel on Tuesday 20th September 1910. The man on the extreme left is W.H. Allen and tenth left, below the word "Motor" is W.A. Stevens. (J. Bennett collection)

The Hallford-Stevens bus D4782 receives mechanical attention in Leicester Road, Quorn. The houses to the right still exist. (D.M. Bailey collection)

Tilling-Stevens AY 2226 at the Brush works after the fitting of the bodywork in December 1912.   (R. Marshall collection)

The Mayor, Walter Coltman, drives the first bus AY 2224, full of local dignitaries, away from the Philharmonic Hall, Southfields Road, after the opening ceremony on 8th January 1913. (J.D. Deakin)

Tilling-Stevens AY 2226 as it appeared in a Brush products catalogue of 1914. Note the "Pay as you enter" sign and the boards showing the Sunday seasonal routes. (J. Bennett collection) conductor. These must have been some of the first buses to carry the notice "pay as you enter'. The completed pair were painted dark green, light green and straw and were registered AY2224 and AY2226.

Wednesday 8th January 1913 was chosen for the opening ceremony but the Town Hall was not available and so the company were indebted to Mr W.B. Paget for the free use of the Philharmonic Hall, in Southfields Road, where over 250 guests assembled at 3 p.m. In the presence of the Mayor and Mayoress, Mr and Mrs W.W. Coltman, Councillor W.F. Charles, chairman of the company, outlined the events of the previous twelve years which culminated in the launch of the buses. Referring to the experiments of 1910 as a "trial canter" and the bus used as a "a rather ramshackle article" he outlined the virtues of the new machines and praised the tenacity of Mr Allen in pursuing the development - "What Mr Allen did not know about buses was not worth knowing". With safety in mind he pointed out that the drivers had passed tests of physical and optical fitness and that each held an R.A.C. certificate.

The Mayor took the wheel of the first bus (AY 2224), full of local ladies and gentlemen, amidst some taunting of the police sergeant as to whether he held a driving licence or not. After photographs had been taken, Mr Allen took the wheel of the second vehicle (AY 2226) following the Mayor's vehicle on a circuit taking in the Market Place, High Street, Great Central Road, Nottingham Road and Clarence Street. The regular drivers then took over, carrying over 270 passengers on the same circuit until about 5 p.m., by which time over 300 persons had taken tea and cakes and been further entertained by records of Sousa's marches played on a gramophone. The local press recorded the event in detail and the *Loughborough Echo* even included a photograph of the first bus, at a time when pictures were not commonplace in newspapers, especially in provincial weeklies.

At its meeting on 6th January the Council granted omnibus drivers' licences to Ernest Black, Mark Huntingdon and Arthur Selby, all resident in Loughborough and it seems likely that these were the company's first employees, the men to whom the responsibility of operating the service fell. A huge crowd had gathered to witness the launch the previous day and a substantial number waited in the

Market Place at 10 a.m. the next morning (9th January) to witness the first departures. The Shepshed-bound bus arrived first but there was no rush to board it and so it departed, only to meet the Mountsorrel bus in Swan Street, where the roadway was so narrow that it was all but impossible to pass, resulting in an order that the buses were to await each other in the Market Place. The Mountsorrel bus returned at 10.56 a.m. well laden but most of the passengers had apparently "lost" their tickets which had to be returned to the driver for re-issue.

In the afternoon, one of the *Echo*'s reporters decided to sample the Shepshed service himself to obtain first-hand information from which he was able to write a substantial column. The journey itself was uneventful, although the buses had apparently brought good luck as far as the weather was concerned, another ideal day, and the vehicle itself created a very good impression, smooth running, with only a gentle swaying motion. At Shepshed, a crowd of youths gathered to torment the driver and make contemptuous remarks about the bus, which they unkindly compared to a hearse, in spite of which a fair number of passengers boarded and were conveyed safely to Loughborough. One gentleman having enquired of the fare, announced his intention to walk almost a mile to Shepshed station and take the train to town, thereby saving himself a half-penny.

The Spring-like weather did not last and on the first Saturday of operation, rain at midday turned to snow and blizzard but the buses continued to run earning the gratitude of Shepshed marketers. A dense fog had descended on the area by Monday and one bus was involved in serious collision with a baker's cart in Leicester Road, receiving damage to the bonnet and causing suspension of the service until Wednesday. The baker, Mr Edwin Fisher, took the company to court and was duly awarded £10 in damages after alleging that the vehicle was speeding; the driver claimed he was travelling at only 10 m.p.h. On the second Saturday, engine lubrication problems caused the withdrawal of one vehicle and the loss of some journeys, much to the disappointment of prospective passengers intending to return home by bus.

The local press gave considerable support, expressing the hope that the "service will receive loyal support" and explaining that "suggestions will be fully considered by the Directors" but there was no shortage of passengers and Mr Allen was forced to set out guidance for bus travellers at busy periods in a letter published in the *Herald* on 23rd January. The essential details are as follows:

1) Queue two abreast, not more than 30 persons, facing the direction the car is coming;
2) Allow passengers to alight first and turn left alongside the car; .
3) Have the exact fare and do not require change;
4) Retain queue as car is loaded and do not crowd the steps;
5) Give longer distance passengers the first opportunity;
6) Do not give the driver stopping instructions in advance, use the bell;
7) Have tickets ready to give up to the driver when alighting.

How well the public responded to Mr Allen's advice is not reported but other difficulties were soon to emerge. The writer of another letter to a newspaper criticized the lack of a rear emergency exit and also the lack of a conductor - jobs were not being created for the working classes, a point alluded to by Mr W.F. Charles in his address at the opening ceremony. In February and March 1913 the Sanitary Committee issued conductors' licences to B. Elliott, F. Padmore, W. Tooley and J. Wain, all of Loughborough. It would seem that these men were the first Road Car conductors although it is much more likely that patronage rather than public pressure secured their employment.

The weather continued to deal a poor hand and on Monday 10th February, in fog so dense that it rendered the single headlamp useless, one of the buses left the road and ended up at a precarious angle in the ditch opposite Wood Lane at Quorn as it tried to make its way to Loughborough on the last journey of the day from Mountsorrel. It was left for the night, but early next morning the fitters were out, digging the soil away from beneath the vehicle and employing the strength of a passing traction engine to haul it back on to the road. The newspaper report of the incident called upon the directors to "look to their laurels" as a result of this "chapter of accidents", somewhat of an exaggeration even if one of the buses had clipped a signpost in the Market Place on the very first day. When the weather did improve, in March, clouds of dust on Ashby Road were blamed on the buses and the road was sprayed with tar as far as Burleigh Brook Park, a pleasure park owned by George Adcock and much frequented for picnics and Sunday School treats.

At the full Council meeting on 3rd March, Councillor F. Stenson questioned the time Mr Allen had given to the affairs of the Road Car Company when he was employed as engineer to run the Electricity undertaking. Although there was no question of Mr Allen being paid by the company for his services it was suggested that he should not be called upon to look at motor-buses which broke down or "tried to take fences in the Quorn country" - a sarcastic reference to the recent accident in an area used by the Quorn Hunt. A motion was phrased stating that officials employed by the council should seek permission to undertake work for private firms but when it was put to the vote it was defeated. Shortly afterwards Mr Allen asked the Electricity Committee of the Council to define his hours of work, which they could not do, not least because they wished him to be available at any hour when necessary, and so the controversy died down as quickly as it had arisen.

Timetables of the services began to appear regularly in the *Loughborough Echo* from June 1913 with six routes offered. Services 1 for Shepshed and 2 for Quorn and Mountsorrel both ran daily; services 3 for Quorn and 4 for Hathern on Thursdays and Saturdays only whilst services 5 for Quorn and Woodhouse Eaves and 6 for Nanpantan were Sundays only. These last numbered services were provided to allow town residents an afternoon out in the country; both villages boasted tearooms and licensed establishments and a number of country walks could begin or end at either. In order to maintain this level of service, both buses were required on Sundays, Thursdays and Saturdays and one on the remaining days of the weeks; thus there was no provision for mechanical failure on the busiest days. During October the Woodhouse Eaves service ceased, followed a week later on 2nd November by that to Nanpantan; the others continued unaltered although the service numbers were removed from the timetables.

A daily parcels delivery service was also provided by the buses, although its organization and advertising were looked after by the Tradesmen's Association who appointed agents in Loughborough, Mountsorrel, Quorn and Shepshed to receive and to distribute the goods carried.

22

The second Annual General Meeting, held on 29th December 1913, was able to look back on a most successful year. Traffic receipts for the eleven months up to November 1913 amounted to £2,158, over 187,000 passengers had been carried and the vehicles had operated 50,000 miles between them. There was some difficulty in accommodating all those wishing to travel on Thursdays, Saturdays and Sundays but patronage on the other days was not too good. To cope with the overloading situation the directors had in view plans to alter the existing vehicle bodies or to rebody the two chassis to increase the seating capacity - neither scheme was carried out. An operating profit of over £309 was declared from which it was proposed to pay a dividend of 5% free of income tax, which would absorb £125 with the balance of £184 being kept in reserve. Loughborough and district had finally got its bus service, bringing more people into the town and the shareholders had every reason to be well satisfied.

Advertisement in the *Loughborough Echo* 4th April 1913

LOUGHBOROUGH ROAD CAR CO., LTD.

Time Table of Services.

JANUARY, 1916, AND UNTIL FURTHER NOTICE.

Leave Loughborough for SHEPSHED.

Monday, Tuesday, Wednesday and Friday, 10 a.m., 12 noon, 2, 4, 6, and 8 p.m.
Thursday, 10 a.m., 12 noon, 1, 2, 3, 4, 5, 6, and 8 p.m.
Saturday, 10 a.m., 12 noon, 1, 2, 3, 4, 5, 6, 7, 8, 9, and 10 p.m.
Sunday, 2, 4, 6, and 8 p.m.
Return Journey from Shepshed half-hour later than above times.

Leave Loughborough for QUORN and MOUNTSORREL.

Monday, Tuesday, Wednesday, Thursday and Friday, 11 a.m., 1, 3, 5, 7, and 9 p.m.
Saturday, 11 a.m., 1, 3, 5, 7, 9, and 11 p.m.
Sunday, 10, 11 a.m., 1, 3, 5, 7, and 9 p.m.
Return Journey from Mountsorrel half-hour later than above times.

Leave Loughborough for QUORN ONLY.

Thursday, 2-30, 4-30, and 6-30 p.m.
Saturday, 2-30, 4-30, 6-30, 8-30, and 10-30 p.m.
Sunday, 10 p.m.
Return Journey from Quorn 15 minutes later than above times.

Leave Loughborough for HATHERN.

Thursday, 2, 4, and 6 p.m.
Saturday, 2, 4, 6, 8, and 10 p.m.
Sunday, 12 noon, and 12-30 p.m.
Return Journey from Hathern 15 minutes later than above times.

This Time Table does not apply to Bank Holidays and other similar occasions, for which special Time Tables will be published as required, and exhibited in the Cars and the Co.'s Notice Boxes at the various termini.

FARES:

Between

Loughborough Market Place and

Hathern	=	=	3d.
Mountsorrel	=	=	3d.
Shepshed	=	=	4d.

With intermediate 1d. stages.

Smoking, Eating, Drinking, Singing or Shouting strictly prohibited.   No Dogs will be carried.
N.B.—NO SERVICE ON CHRISTMAS DAY.

For all other particulars and general information see small Time Tables, which are supplied free of charge. The Conductors on the Cars will issue Time Tables to legitimate enquirers.

January 1916 timetable leaflet reproduced by courtesy of Mr J.D. Deakin

DEVELOPMENTS

The new year did not begin well for the Road Car Company. On Saturday 21st February 1914 the 10.30 p.m. bus to Quorn left promptly with a full load including standing passengers, with others on the platform and steps alongside driver Reginald Barrowcliff. A little over a mile south of Loughborough, just beyond Bull in the Hollow Farm, the bus collided with a horsedrawn waggonette killing the horse instantly. The shaft of the waggonette penetrated the side of the bus just behind the driver, seriously injuring Mrs Hannah Wykes. The vehicle proceeded to the Doctor's house at Quorn, then to the hospital in Loughborough and finally to the Police Station!

In April, at the County Court with Judge Moore-Cann presiding, Henry Roe, cab proprietor of Regent Street, Loughborough, sought to sue the Road Car for £40, representing the value of the horse and damage to the waggonette and harness. Mr G. Johnson, the driver, gave evidence that he recognised the bus by its light and heard the vehicle's gong sound; he alleged that the bus was going at 20 m.p.h. in the middle of the road and that he was on his correct side of the road. Johnson was knocked out, the horse killed and the empty waggonette finished up four feet from the kerb, a fact confirmed by Harry Brutnell, a Road Car driver who came upon the scene. Eleven days later the case continued with J.A. Compston, K.C., opening the case in defence of the Road Car, pointing out that it was not negligent to be in the middle of the road and that blood from the horse was in the bus's half of the road! The Road Car driver stated that the waggonette was "running square" and that he knew that an accident was inevitable; he braked but due to the curve of the road the nearside wheels mounted the footpath and he stopped within twenty yards. Six of the passengers who were on the platform gave evidence in support of the driver, one suggesting that the waggonette driver pulled on the wrong rein whilst at least one pedestrian said that the waggonette was not under proper control.

The jury, who according to the report, did not all take their task very seriously, asked for clarification of various points before returning their verdict finding the waggonette driver negligent. It might seem a little strange that such a case should have ever come to court but it is suggested that there was an element of competition between the waggonettes and the buses which might account for what could be seen as an attempt to put the Road Car in its place.

A second sale of shares was organized for 6th February which raised another £533 and added twenty persons to the list of shareholders, half of whom were ladies, including the wives of some of the existing shareholders and a number of spinster school teachers. This was to be the last share offer, although there were a number of transactions between holders later, and brought the capital invested in the company to a total of £3,033.

Later in the month, from 23rd February, the Mountsorrel terminus was moved from The Green to the Railway Bridge at the northern end of the village and the fare from Loughborough was reduced by 1d. to 3d. In March the Council granted the company an omnibus licence for a third vehicle and permission for a 1,000 gallon petrol tank which was to be cased in six inches of Portland cement.

The reason for these preparations was clear to the sharp-sighted as early as 30th January when a newspaper report of a Shepshed U.D.C. meeting revealed that the Road Car had requested that certain trees be cut back as a double-decker bus would soon be on the road, a request that was refused as no danger was anticipated. The new vehicle arrived in time for Easter and was sampled on Wednesday 8th April by local dignitaries, including one "Bohemian", columnist in the *Loughborough Echo*. He was most enthusiastic and wished to dispel fears about the upper-deck, stating that he had travelled on such vehicles in London and that he would only be inside this summer if the top deck was full. This was a "further bid for public support and done in the right direction".

Bohemian's promise was well placed for a particularly fine vehicle had been obtained at a cost of £868 with chassis by Daimler and the body by Brush. The chassis was of the more conventional type with a gearbox, clutch and shaft and worm transmission, almost certainly a CD model with 40 h.p. 5.7 litre engine and a 14 feet wheelbase. Brush provided an excellent, if slightly unusual, body which had more in common with their single-deck designs of the time.

The lower panels did not taper in to the chassis at the bottom, giving a wider body, allowing for transverse seats, although the saloon had some longitudinal seats and accommodated eighteen persons. A cab screen was provided, fully glazed, with the driver's side window unglazed. There was access on the nearside of the vehicle only to a bench seat for the driver and three passengers. The open top deck, reached by a curved staircase, extended unusually part way over the cab and had seats for twenty-two, all facing forward, giving a total capacity of 43 persons, well in excess of the 34 then usually carried by a double-decker. The vehicle was finished in a dark green, light green and straw, much of which was hidden by extensive advertisements; it was registered AY 3240. The company and Mr Allen, who almost certainly designed the body, had every right to be very proud of their new acquisition.

A large advertisement in the *Loughborough Echo* outlined an ambitious programme of services for the Easter period, 12th to 14th April inclusive; clearly it was intended to make the most of the new vehicle and the weekend was apparently blessed with summer-like weather. On Easter Monday the Shepshed route was served hourly, Mountsorrel every two hours and there were six return trips to Woodhouse Eaves and twelve to Nanpantan. A week later, 20th April was Loughborough Race Day, a day that was regarded locally as an annual holiday when huge numbers of people from all over the county enjoyed a day out at what was correctly called the Quorn Hunt Steeplechases. The course was about a mile north of the town, adjacent to the Soar Navigation but the Road Car company concentrated its efforts in getting people into Loughborough, offering an hourly service from both Shepshed and Mountsorrel, except in the mid-afternoon, augmented with a number of extras to Quorn which were to operate if required.

The evening services to Woodhouse Eaves and Nanpantan were advertised weekly from June and operated on both Wednesdays and Sundays but in spite of the extra work the timetable could usually be maintained by two vehicles, leaving one as a spare or for duplication of busy timings.

The company's passengers were not always as well behaved as one might have imagined and a public apology from two of them was printed on the front page of the *Loughborough Echo* on 27th March.

27

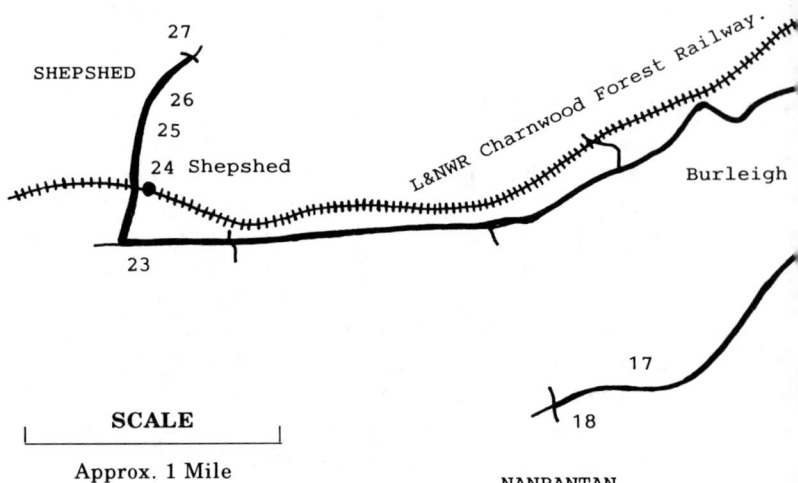

THE LOUGHBOROUGH ROAD CAR COMPANY LIMITED.

ROUTE MAP

32

HATHERN

DISHLEY

Garendon Hall

THORP

27

SHEPSHED

26

25

24 Shepshed

23

L&NWR Charnwood Forest Railway.

Burleigh

17

18

NANPANTAN

SCALE

Approx. 1 Mile

STOPPING PLACES	
1 Barrow Street	17 School House
2 Central Road	18 Longcliffe Hotel
3 Beeches Road	19 Frederick Street
4 Cemetery	20 Radmoor Road
5 Woodhouse Lane	21 Cumberland Road
6 Barrow Lane	22 Thorpe Lane
7 White Horse	23 Cross Roads
8 Wood Lane	24 Station Bridge
9 Howcliffe Road	25 Ring Fence
10 Company Cottages	26 Garendon Road
11 Terminus	27 Bull Ring
12 Station	28 Derby Square
13 Church	29 Bridge Street
14 Bulls Head	30 Station
15 Pear Tree	31 Thorpe Lane
16 The Widenings	32 The Green

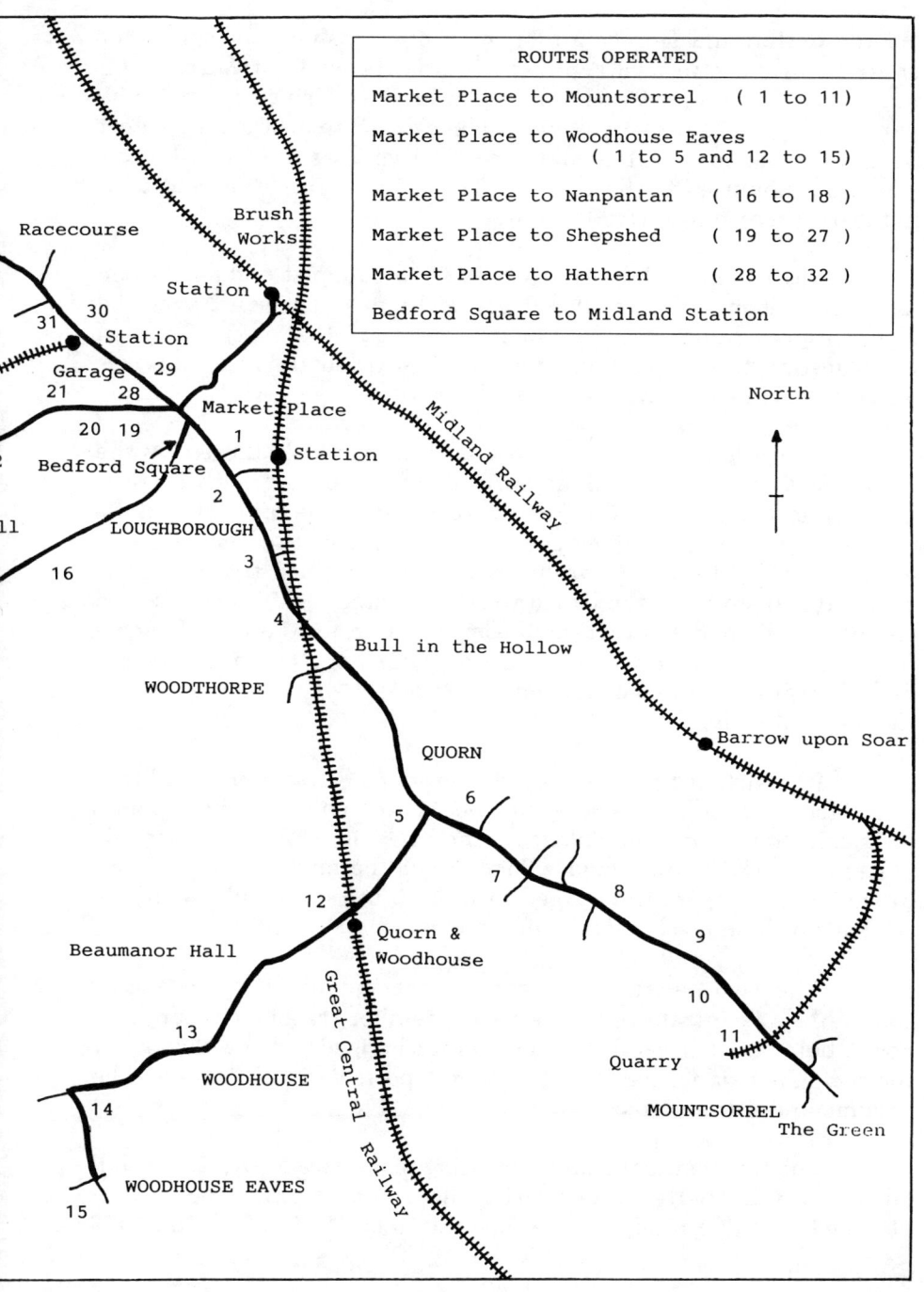

ROUTES OPERATED

Market Place to Mountsorrel (1 to 11)

Market Place to Woodhouse Eaves
(1 to 5 and 12 to 15)

Market Place to Nanpantan (16 to 18)

Market Place to Shepshed (19 to 27)

Market Place to Hathern (28 to 32)

Bedford Square to Midland Station

North

Racecourse

Brush
Works

Station

Station

Garage

Market Place

Bedford Square

Station

LOUGHBOROUGH

Bull in the Hollow

WOODTHORPE

QUORN

Barrow upon Soar

Beaumanor Hall

Quorn &
Woodhouse

Great Central Railway

Midland Railway

WOODHOUSE

WOODHOUSE EAVES

Quarry

MOUNTSORREL

The Green

George Cotton and Horace Miller, both of Shepshed, apologized for their behaviour in two separate incidents on 21st March and undertook not to repeat such conduct in future. The company for its part gave notice that they intended to put a stop to disorderly conduct on their buses and stated that a set of Bye-laws and Regulations would be submitted to the Board of Trade for confirmation and that, in future, proceedings would be taken.

August Bank Holiday 1914 fell on 3rd August and once again many extra journeys were offered, especially to Woodhouse Eaves and Nanpantan, as much as a half-hourly service to the latter village on the Tuesday though the advertisement warned that the services would be curtailed in the event of bad weather.

These happy events were completely overshadowed by the outbreak of war with Germany, officially announced on 4th August, but a situation that was far from unexpected. The most immediate effect on the company was the impressment of the Daimler bus chassis for military use, probably as a lorry since the body was removed and stored at the Brush works. A sum of £597 was received for the chassis but this was small compensation for the loss of such a fine vehicle at a time when there was little hope of a replacement being obtained; indeed its departure was being blamed for the company's difficulties as late as 1918.

In a further tightening up of operations it was announced that from Monday 24th August the cars would stop only at certain points in Loughborough and the villages. Intermediate stops at reasonable places outside the towns and villages would be made by request but intending passengers were urged to wait on the left-hand side of the road and only on level or downhill sections.

The two seasonal services were removed when a new timetable was introduced on 11th September, rather earlier than usual, but the other services remained unchanged. A few days later the company paid for damage to two lamp posts but unfortunately the circumstances are not recorded.

The third annual general meeting took place at the Town Hall on Monday 28th December 1914 and seems to have been well attended. Traffic receipts were reported to be £2645 of which £1966 was consumed by operating costs and £466 for depreciation of vehicles and equipment leaving a balance of £237. It was revealed that, after the double-decker had entered service, both of the Tilling-Stevens saloons had been fully overhauled, a process which took a total of six weeks. At some stage the slide-down side windows of the bodies were fixed and opening top ventilators provided instead, presumably because the glass declined to stay in the closed position. The radiators were replaced with the later style featuring, in large letters, *Tilling-Stevens Petrol Electric*, usually fitted to the TS3 model introduced in 1914. Destination boxes were also fitted on to the front edge of the roof of each bus, containing a linen roller blind which could be set to display the names of the places served. These are still a feature of modern vehicles but in 1914 they were quite new! It cannot be confirmed that these modifications were undertaken in the Spring of that year but it seems most likely that they were.

In what can only be described as an ill-advised move the directors recommended a dividend of 10%, at a cost considerably in excess of the profit for the year and thus drawing on the previous balance and making no provision for the reserve fund, a point which Councillor A.E. Shepherd was quick to point out. A further £20 was voted to the Prince of Wales Fund, a national relief fund, an announcement which brought spontaneous applause. Mr F.H. Allsop, President of the Tradesmen's Association, congratulated the directors on the returns; his members, most of whom were shareholders, wanted people brought into the town; now they had this and a profit as well. Mr A. Hibbins, of the long-established family of boot makers, suggested that each of the directors receive £5 per annum for their services but Councillor Shepherd, clearly unimpressed by the euphoria, insisted that it should be for the previous year's work only, after which the motion was carried. Mr E.H. Deane, an accountant, suggested that as Mr Allen undertook all the duties of a manager he should be given a present of £25 as a consulting fee and this was readily agreed. In reply, Mr Allen said that he derived considerable satisfaction from the success of the company but it could be made into a much better concern if a full-time manager were appointed.

In February 1915 the company's office was transferred from Mr Allen's house to rented premises within Lloyd's Bank Chambers at the corner of Market Place and High Street and therefore adjacent to the main stopping place used by the buses.

The Corporation Electricity Department, of which Mr Allen was both engineer and manager, was not doing as well financially as it ought; it drew on, rather than contributed to, the town rates. In an age where electricity in the home, office and factory is almost universal it must be remembered that gas fulfilled most of these functions, including street lighting. Mr Allen's response to the difficulties was a detailed report presented to the Electricity Committee on 9th February 1915. Amongst his suggestions as to the use of electricity for lighting and for domestic heating and cooking, came the first details of a new development for the Road Car, an electric bus.

Edison Accumulators Ltd had developed the battery-powered electric bus, based on a GMC 2-ton chassis imported from the United States. This was propelled by a 6 h.p. electric motor supplied by batteries placed under the seats or in some cases beneath the chassis. The drive to the rear wheels was provided by a system of shafts and finally by silent roller side chains; a maximum speed of 12 m.p.h. could be achieved and about fifty miles travelled before recharging. Three minute boost charges during the day and a night-time recharge for five hours were both necessary.

Many of the vehicles had bodies built by Brush and that company was involved in the production of battery-powered vehicles for municipal applications up to the 1960s. Southend and South Shields introduced such buses during 1914; York, West Bromwich and Loughborough in 1915. The Road Car vehicle had a twenty-two seat front-entrance body by Brush and was registered AY 4058. The Sanitary Committee granted a licence for the new bus on 17th February and "Bohemian" gave details in his newspaper column published only two days later, describing the venture as "an enterprise of great pith and moment".

A horse bus had operated to and from the Midland Station since at least 1871 in which year it was reported that Mr John Warren of Baxtergate had just completed a very well appointed twelve-seat vehicle for Mr Greenwood of the King's Head Hotel, in time for the annual Dispensary [Hospital] Ball in January. Many years later (in 1958) a former driver Mr J. North recalled that the bus operated about twelve times a day from the hotel yard to the Midland

and Great Central stations and also that another like it, operated by Mr J. Moss served the Charnwood Forest (L&NWR) station.

It was the Midland station route that was chosen for the new electric bus, beginning at Bedford Square, proceeding to the Market Place and then by way of Church Gate and Nottingham Road to the Midland Station, a distance of almost one mile. The *Loughborough Echo* of 2nd July carried an advertisement stating that the route would commence shortly and this was followed by one a week later giving details of the service, which was to begin on Monday 12th July and operate every 20 minutes between 8 a.m. and 10 p.m., the fare to be one penny. The intention to operate every 15 minutes in the future was expressed but experience must have dictated otherwise as a subsequent advertisement showed that from Monday 19th July the service was designed to connect with specific train departures and arrivals, with thirty return journeys being offered.

The introduction was not without its own controversy for at a Council Meeting on 26th July, Councillor Dickens asked a question about a charging station that had been fixed in Bedford Square, to establish whether it was at the expense of the Road Car Company or the ratepayers. He was informed that the company paid £23 a year for the plant plus the cost of the electricity for charging the bus and the present writer is most grateful to the Councillor as he has caused the location of the booster station to be put on record.

The two seasonal services to Woodhouse Eaves and Nanpantan were not advertised at all during 1915, and possibly did not operate, but extra services were provided for Shepshed Wakes on 4th to 6th July with an hourly frequency and additional Sunday services were announced to Garendon Camp and to the Cemetery, the latter being on the southern edge of the town.

At a meeting of the Sanitary Committee on 2nd July it was alleged that the company was using unlicensed staff and allowing its vehicles to be dangerously overloaded, so the Town Clerk was instructed to write to the company. In reply the company pointed out that it had recently engaged a number of girls as conductors to release male labour for war work and there was a considerable delay in obtaining the necessary licences and badges from the Council. Dorothy Harris, Rose Clarke, Nancy Wootton and Sara Stothard were

33

granted conductor's licences and is thought that all of these ladies were Road Car employees; the last named certainly was. As a result of these delays it was agreed that such applications need not go to the full council for approval.

On the subject of overcrowding the company simply pointed out that the public rushed the vehicles, giving the staff no opportunity to control the loadings. It was most unfortunate that a letter had also been received from the Reverend A.W. Curwood complaining that on 24th August one bus had been so overloaded and driven by such an inexperienced driver that it swerved and overbalanced dangerously as it progressed. The Inspector of Hackneys was asked to look out for overcrowding and he reported that everything was satisfactory a month later. An accident did occur on Saturday 28th September when a bus on its way from Hathern collided with a motor-cycle combination on Derby Road about three-quarters of a mile from the town. The motor-cyclist and his two passengers were taken by ambulance to hospital; at least on this occasion the bus was not held to be at fault.

The Chairman, Mr A.E. Armstrong again presided over the annual general meeting, the fourth, at the Town Hall on Thursday 30th December 1915. Traffic receipts amounted to £2808 but operating expenses had risen sharply to £2188 with £474 written off for depreciation leaving a profit of only £165; a dividend of 5% was paid. A major shock was the resignation of Mr W.H. Allen and his replacement as a director by Mr G.P. Jones, a retired gentleman. Considerable concern was expressed at Mr Allen's departure; he had always been the driving force behind any moves the company made but in spite of one shareholder telling the board that it was deliberately keeping them "in the dark", no answers were given.

It is easy to speculate what had happened because it was clear that the electric bus was not a success and the scheme had been of Mr Allen's design. The vehicles at South Shields earned 6.55d. a mile and those at York 9.88d. but this was not enough to meet the running charges and depreciation. West Bromwich experienced great problems with the batteries, which had to be overhauled in London, and everywhere the vehicles were ridiculed for their ponderous progress. Loughborough's electric bus, operating only sixty miles a day, would need to average ten passengers on each journey to earn

10d a mile, which was probably insufficient even if anything like that number of passengers travelled. The fare was increased to 1½d. and reduced again to 1d. on 29th December 1915, resulting in more passengers being carried. In spite of the problems, shareholders were assured that whilst the service was at an experimental stage it was a permanent operation. The slow speed of the bus and the steep gradients on the country routes meant that it could not hope to succeed on the other services; there was little choice but to persevere.

The bus almost became a lorry in July 1916 when the Electrical Engineer established that the company were willing to sell the chassis for £700 but he decided to investigate a new chassis. In the event neither purchase was proceeded with and coal continued to be transported by horses and carts to the electricity works until two steam waggons were purchased in 1919.

There is later confirmation that Mr Allen did resign on a point of principle because in a September 1916 letter of reference for mechanic Mr H.H. Single, he refers to severing his connections with the Road Car company and to Mr Single having to take over as acting manager. A new manager, Mr Orlando Rolls of Macclesfield was introduced to the shareholders at the annual general meeting but in less than a year he was called up for military service.

Other vehicle news was much better, although one Tilling-Stevens had been used for parts to keep the other on the road, spares had finally been acquired to enable both of them to operate. In addition a new chassis had been purchased from the McCurd Lorry Manufacturing Co. Ltd of Hayes, Middlesex, a four ton chassis with a 4-cylinder 40 h.p. petrol engine. It had a 14 ft 6 ins wheelbase and a 5 ft 6 ins track and, being of very similar dimensions to the Daimler, it was fitted with the body from that vehicle, by Brush, with the intention of having it in service in mid-January. The vehicle was registered AY 4984 and a licence was granted by the Sanitary Committee but otherwise its entry into the fleet seems to have gone unrecorded in the press, in which much of the column space was devoted to the progress of the war and the war effort.

The company had every reason to begin 1916 with optimism; they had a full-time manager and a full fleet strength of four vehicles again. Timetables show that a good level of service was being provided, including a shortlived Sunday operation to Hathern, although there are some errors apparent in the advertising at this time including the omission of a Saturday service to Mountsorrel.

Apart from the horse-drawn waggonettes the Road Car buses had not experienced any competition along their routes until March 1916 when the Leicester Watch Committee granted licences to the Midland Motor Omnibus Co. Ltd to ply for hire between Foundry Square in the city and Loughborough and the service was duly advertised. This new company, which had no connections with the similarly named Birmingham & Midland Motor Omnibus Co. Ltd (the "Midland Red"), had a registered office in Northampton and set up operations in Leicester early in 1916 using a small fleet of Straker-Squire double-deck buses, accommodated at premises in Oxford Street. Routes from Leicester reached Hinckley, Loughborough and Barrow-upon-Soar in 1916 whilst by 1918 additional routes were operated to Thurmaston, Anstey, Syston and Enderby but it may be that competition from the expansionist Midland Red in 1922 forced the earlier company's withdrawal.

The Road Car company took the threat of a competitor very seriously and letters were sent to Loughborough Council's Highway Committee and to the Sanitary Committee, as well as to the Board of Trade in London. The new service had not begun operation in May 1916 but on 17th May the Sanitary Committee recommended the granting of a licence to Midland as they felt that they had no power to do otherwise. However, the opposition seems to have worked as Midland commenced operations between Leicester and Barrow-upon-Soar instead. No application was received at Loughborough until 1918 when two vehicles were allowed and by 1919 the Leicester to Loughborough service was operating on Wednesday, Saturday and Sunday whilst from May 1922 Parr's Garage (later to become Leicester and District) were operating daily and Midland had disappeared.

A large advertisement in the *Loughborough Echo* of 14th April 1916 stated that the company "Beg to Announce that the Full Service is now Running" and offered an Easter Programme with ten journeys to Nanpantan on Good Friday 21st April and special services on Easter Monday and Tuesday on all routes (except to Hathern) including both Nanpantan and Woodhouse Eaves. Beginning in June

36

the Nanpantan route also operated on weekday evenings, leaving Loughborough at 7.15 p.m. and returning at 9.30 p.m. as well as on Wednesday afternoons, on which day the outward evening journey ran at 6.30 p.m. At a time when business prospects seemed good and the fleet was performing well the national shortage of petrol dealt a bitter blow to the company from which it never really recovered.

In addition the electric bus was not doing well. Bohemian commented on the lack of support in his newspaper column and the Electricity Committee refused to give a reduction in the price of night-time power for charging. The hire of a charging generator was terminated in May 1916 after which the bus was charged each night in the Electricity Works.

A new, reduced timetable was issued in August showing a much lower level of service on most days, except on Thursdays and Saturdays when the markets were held and demand was at its highest. The August Bank Holiday was postponed, such was the need for the town's products in the war effort and the holiday was eventually declared between 28th September and 1st October. In September the company advised its patrons that due to the shortage of petrol it would not be possible to give the usual level of service on penny fares and that these would only be taken after longer distance passengers were seated.

The fifth annual general meeting on Friday 29th December 1916 was a much more tumultuous affair than usual, not least because the company made a substantial loss on the year's trading. Traffic receipts were £2489, over £300 down on the previous year, in spite of the double-deck being in service, whilst costs had risen to £2374 which, when depreciation was taken into account, left a loss of £535. Seeking to explain the situation, Mr A.E. Armstrong, the chairman, noted that the public had not taken to the electric bus and it was not a success and that even though the new double-decker was running well, petrol supplies had only been half the normal level for the past four months. Mr W.F. Charles arrived as the meeting was about to close and began to question and criticize the actions of the Board, maintaining that the losses resulted from the too severe depreciation of the buses, 20% per annum on the motor-buses and 15% on the electric bus. He recommended that no reserve fund should be kept and that the company should buy new buses; if these points were discussed, nothing was recorded and no action was taken. In conclusion it was noted that fares must rise in the new year.

Good times and bad times. Above: advertising the Easter programme (*Loughborough Echo* 14th April 1916). Below: two years later, capitalizing on a necessity (*Loughborough Echo* 19th July 1918)

The superb Daimler double-decker posed with crew in full uniform at the Bull Ring, Shepshed in the spring of 1914.   (S. Evans)

A magnificent rear view of the Daimler in 1914 before it entered service.   Note the plethora of advertisements for businesses owned by Road Car directors. (R. Marshall collection)

The Daimler double-decker with a party of local gentlemen.   The occasion and location remain a mystery. (J. Clarke collection)

The Road Car Edison battery bus AY 4058 is thought to have been identical to this one owned by Lancaster Corporation and seen taking a booster battery charge between journeys.   (T.W.W. Knowles)

Lancaster Edison battery bus B 5981, in original condition, photographed at the Brush works before delivery.   (J. Bennett collection)

One of the pair of Tilling-Stevens buses, in rebuilt form and carrying a gas bag on the roof, refilling outside the Maypole Dairy, Market Place, in 1918. (R. Marshall collection)

Trent Tilling-Stevens CH 1769, one of the vehicles allocated to Loughborough. It is seen outside the Rushes garage, probably in 1921, on the Nottingham route. The driver is Mr Frank Strawford. (J. Clarke collection)

PROBLEMS AND SOLUTIONS.

An advertisement in the public notices column of the *Loughborough Echo* advised patrons that the bus service would be further curtailed from 22nd January 1917, when a new timetable would be issued. There was also a paper shortage at the time and the weekly publication of the timetable in the newspaper, which had been a feature since 1913, ceased, leaving little evidence of the level of service offered. Leaflets giving details of the timetable were available from the office in Lloyd's Bank Chambers and passengers were henceforward expected to obtain copies or read the notice boards; the newspaper advertisement also referred readers to these for full details.

During the Easter weekend in mid-April special services to Nanpantan and Woodhouse Eaves were advertised, although the holiday was blighted with heavy rain and some snow. At Whitsuntide, at the end of May, extra services were also announced. It seems that the company made a special effort to provide services for these brief holidays, possibly hoarding supplies of petrol to make these profitable operations possible, since there were few other opportunities for the townsfolk to engage in any relaxation in the countryside. In June the situation was even worse; no services were operated on Tuesday or Friday from the beginning of the month and a few days later services were further curtailed by withdrawing most of the morning journeys, except on Thursdays.

However the company announced rather cautiously that the full service would resume on Monday 22nd October 1917 and that new timetables were available at the office. The reason behind this optimism was not because of improved petrol supplies but because the buses had been converted to run on gas. The ever ingenious and industrious foreman-mechanic Mr. H.H. Single, who worked for the company throughout most of its existence, had contrived to convert both of the ageing Tilling-Stevens saloons to run on coal gas stored in huge canvas bags attached to the roof of the buses. Barton Brothers of Beeston, near Nottingham, were pioneers of this form of propulsion and more locally Wakefield's Garage of Mountsorrel advertised in September 1917 that they could fit coal gas containers to both lorries and cars.

The essential principle is quite simple, a mixture of gas and air is supplied to the cylinders of the engine, which is almost directly equivalent to the petrol vapour and air mix normally present. The spark plugs ignite the mixture in the usual way, making the conversion of a petrol engine fairly simple. Petrol was commonly used to start the cold engine, switching over to gas after a few minutes; then the only problem was reduced power, usually in the order of 30%, quite considerable on hilly routes. The two Road Car buses were now powered by engines fuelled with gas which in turn drove electric motors to drive the vehicles, gas-electrics no less!

The Council's Gas Committee noted at its meeting on 14th September that arrangements had been made for a supply of gas for driving purposes for the Road Car Company but this was soon to cause trouble. The supply standard was positioned in an archway beneath the buildings on the north side of the Market Place. A canvas supply hose was linked to the bus, which stood in front of the premises of the Maypole Dairy Company for the seven minutes it took to inflate the gas bag after each journey. The Maypole company, owned by Sir William Watson, manufactured margarine and sold it in over one thousand shops across the country, reaping huge profits whilst butter was in short supply during the Great War. In November the Dairy company objected to the gas standard being next to its premises and was supported by Police Superintendent Agar who said that the buses using it caused a traffic obstruction. Initially a public supply was offered but this ceased as a result of the complaints. The Gas Committee denied responsibility, saying that the installation was the property of the Road Car Company who had in fact invested £118 for its provision.

Further reference to the problem was made at the sixth annual general meeting on Friday 28th December and in the local press in early January 1918. The Gas Manager had been asked to find an alternative site for the installation but the Road Car Company complained that if it were moved to their Derby Road premises twenty minutes would be lost each hour during the service for gas filling and

40

that an hourly service could not be maintained.   A decision was deferred at various Gas Committee meetings but after another letter from the Maypole Dairy Company in May 1918 the Road Car and the Dairy's representatives met and by June the standard was situated at the Derby Road garage.   Shortly afterwards the company placed its only advertisement for 1918, for a Public Gas Charging Station, at the garage, open daily from 8 a.m. to 9 p.m.

The annual general meeting heard that the traffic receipts were down to £1838 for the year and that costs amounted to £2033, a most unsatisfactory situation, the actual loss being £406.   The explanation by Mr Armstrong was clear.   In 1915 the company had received 250 gallons of petrol a week and this had been gradually reduced until in March 1917 it had fallen to a mere 80 gallons.   Since the two buses began running on gas only a month before the end of the financial year the improvements in returns by operating a full service could not yet be appreciated.

If the reporting is accurate, the tone of the meeting was not at all critical of the Directors or the operation of the company, most speakers praising the efforts of all concerned in working in such difficult conditions and expressing confidence in the future, once the war was over.   The Chairman was congratulated by Mr A.J. Pilsbury (director and shareholder) on negotiating the sale of the electric bus at a profit of £43.   Mr Armstrong had been instrumental in selling the vehicle to Derby Corporation Tramways during April 1917 for £839, a very good price, since it cost £1011 new, two years before.   Derby Corporation put the vehicle into service on the Mansfield Road route to Chester Green which until then had been worked by horse buses. The former Road Car bus lasted until 1923 when its batteries were worn out and it was sold for scrap in December 1925.

Many of the events of 1918 were not recorded fully until the annual general meeting at the end of the year, but the travelling public were only too well aware of the situation faced by the Road Car Company, even if they had little sympathy with the concern and the wholly unsatisfactory service it was able to provide.   On 25th January, the foreman-mechanic Mr H.H. Single resigned after four years with the company during which time he had been relied upon to keep the vehicles running in spite of the shortages imposed by wartime conditions.   A new man, William Croson, was appointed but he was clearly less than impressed with the fleet in his charge as he closed the whole operation down for three months whilst the vehicles were overhauled. Spares were very difficult to obtain, especially for the Tilling-Stevens buses which had been obsolete since 1914 when a new model had been introduced. No doubt the makers were also more fully engaged in war work than bus construction. Petrol restrictions became very severe in the Spring of 1918 and the price had increased by four times the 1913 cost, 2s. 10d. a gallon compared to 7d. A consequence of this was the sale of the McCurd double-decker as it did not run on coal gas. The vehicle was sold at a loss of £148 on its written-down value and must therefore have only realised about £350, less than half of its purchase price just two years earlier. The purchaser is not known but one possible customer is the Ortona Motor Company Ltd of Cambridge which acquired an unidentified McCurd double-decker in 1918. The reasoning behind the decision to sell was rather dubious and was to prove particularly regrettable only a few weeks later.

The *Loughborough Herald* of 4th July 1918 carried a front-page photograph of one of the Tilling-Stevens saloons poised over a ditch with its front end crushed by a tree and the collapsed gas bag hanging limply down the side of the bodywork - a very sorry sight. The 5 p.m. bus to Quorn on Tuesday 25th June had come to grief descending the hill towards the Bull in the Hollow, ironically a section of road along which a number of accidents had occurred to Road Car vehicles over the years. Sadly, the driver died in hospital on 28th June, giving rise to an inquest on 3rd July which revealed all the details of the accident. The bus had made a slightly zig-zag progress along Leicester Road, according to a passenger, Mr J. Boyer of Quorn, but this became much worse after the railway bridge over the Great Central railway, and finally the bus ran into the side of the road and hit a tree. The driver got off and lay in the road complaining of severe pains in his stomach, caused by impact with the steering wheel of the bus; he was taken to hospital. The conductor, Roland Clarke, aged 16, gave evidence saying that the driver had told him, after the accident, that he could not control the vehicle; he pulled the steering wheel, but it had no effect.

The company's manager, William Croson and a driver, Walter Tollington, gave evidence of the good condition of the vehicle. Drivers were instructed to check their vehicle at the chief stopping places and to try to avoid potholes in the road. This was an impossible task due to the appalling condition of the roads, indeed one of the jury had been thrown from his bicycle at the point of the accident the previous evening. The bus had been examined that day, after which it had done 52 miles. The cause of the steering failure was that the three bolts holding the cap of the steering arm had sheared off; the metal cap had been retrieved by a lady pedestrian. A verdict of accidental death was recorded on Thomas Sparks, aged 46, who had been driving for only three months, the cause of his death being internal rupture and peritonitis. The notorious condition of the road was held to blame and the company exonerated. It was also noted, in another newspaper account of the accident that this was not the same bus that ran backwards at Quarry Hill in Shepshed.

Although the company had not been held to blame for the accident, the fact remained that there was now only one serviceable vehicle, AY 2224, the bus that had inaugurated the service in 1913. It continued to work the routes alone, a task no doubt aided by spare parts from its sister vehicle which was beyond economic repair. The Insurers paid the company for the vehicle and, this with the sale of the double-decker contributed £680 to the accounts for the year. There were probably many occasions when the company could not meet its obligation to provide a service at all and the prospect of the bus failing in service when carrying passengers was daunting as they expected to be carried to their destinations. The mechanical staff, at the garage, had no means of reaching the stranded vehicle or of towing it in if roadside repairs proved impractical. In late July the company obtained the registration AY 5956 for a Relyante car, purchased it seems to overcome the worst of the difficulties outlined above. At a cost of only £80 it must have been an old vehicle although its actual age is not known. It was officially described as a brake and landaulette in a yellow and green livery and was initially licensed for trade purposes and as a public conveyance, although this reference is deleted in the motor taxation records. Relyante built cars, largely to the French De Dion design, in London, from as early as 1903 and it was a 15 or 20 h.p. model that joined the fleet.

During the last three months of 1918 Loughborough suffered an influenza epidemic which resulted in the schools being closed and caused the death of 89 people. It was as if the war, which officially ended with the signing of the Armistice on 11th November, had not done enough to demoralize the population of the town. The seventh and last annual general meeting of the Road Car Company took place on Friday 28th December at the Town Hall. Mr T.W. Bailey was now chairman as Mr Armstrong had been prevented from continuing by the loss of staff from his own business. Traffic receipts had dropped to £1138 but with costs at £1774, a large loss of £805 had been incurred, which, with the losses of the previous two years, gave a total deficit of £1690; the company was in a parlous position. The events of the year, detailed above, were outlined but it was clear that the company could not continue in its present state. By this time services were operated only on Thursdays, Saturdays and Sundays. Mr J. Deakin, a shareholder and the proprietor of the *Loughborough Echo,* proposed that the meeting be adjourned and that a committee of inspection be set up to investigate the situation along with the auditors. This was agreed and Messrs A.E.Armstrong, J. Deakin and F.G. Fleeman, the original company secretary, were appointed.

Mr Armstrong was in the chair at the adjourned meeting on Monday 13th January owing to Mr. Bailey being ill and a large number of shareholders were present for the proceedings. The report outlined two proposals, either to go into voluntary liquidation or to raise further capital to purchase two new buses. The chairman, inviting discussion, made his own position clear - he advocated the purchase of three new buses! Liquidation would mean that much of the capital would be lost along with the management's knowledge and experience; the second option called for a contribution of 13s. 4d. per share to raise the new capital of £2000. It was stated that this would allow the new buses to be purchased and a full service operated with every prospect that the company would do well in the favourable post-war conditions and be able to compensate the participating shareholders. Councillor H. Clemerson felt that the committee had not given enough information; it seemed to him that the new buses would be too expensive to buy for operation by a company that was too big for the directors, but too small to pay a skilled manager, a concise and astute summary of the true situation. Mr G. Tilley suggested the bold approach of appointing a skilled manager on a good salary with commission of 5% of the profits but his proposal was not seconded. A proposal that the company be sold as a going concern, not exactly an appropriate term, was moved by Mr H.H. Speight and was seconded by Mr J. Widdowson. Only one shareholder voted against the proposal although a number abstained; the Loughborough Road Car Company was approaching its end.

The *Loughborough Echo* carried details of the sale of the company in an advertisement on 17th January, in response to which tenders had to reach the secretary, Mr A.E. Clarke on or before 29th January. Nothing was published immediately but the *Herald* of the 6th February recorded details of an interview with Mr J.C. Moth, a director of the Trent Motor Traction Company Ltd of Derby. The article pointed out that a number of local gentlemen were seeking to make a new start by raising capital in the town to enable them to reconstruct the company. It went on to outline the progress of the Trent company. Trent had sixteen Tilling-Stevens saloons and services from Derby to Ashbourne, Burton, Melbourne, Mansfield, Nottingham and Alfreton, which, with others gave a total of nine routes, with four garages and a repair works. Mr Moth stated that his company would seek to fulfil the objectives of the Road Car, to bring people into the town of Loughborough, rather than to take them to larger places. It would use four or five new vehicles at a cost of £1250 each; these were already on order and would be delivered long before a new order could be expected.

The Trent argument was certainly persuasive and it was almost inevitable that the Directors would accept it as there was none of the risk associated with forming a new company; the interests of the shareholders would be protected and the district provided with a good bus service again.

The Loughborough Road Car Company, Limited, Loughborough,

Accounts for the Twelve Months ended 30th November, 1918.

Revenue Account.

Dr.	£	s.	d.	Cr.		£	s.	d.
To General Establishment Charges and				By Traffic Receipts		1138	7	8
Management	404	8	2	„ Advertisements Receivable		2	0	0
„ Running Charges	1219	10	9	„ Rent Receivable		9	19	6
„ Repairs and Maintenance ...	151	3	1	„ Loss (see Balance Sheet)		805	16	3
„ Amounts written off	181	1	5					
	£1956	3	5			£1956	3	5

Balance Sheet.

	£	s.	d.		£	s.	d.	£	s.	d.
CAPITAL—				Cash at Bankers and in hand ...				211	11	3
Authorised—5000 Shares of £1 each ..	5000	0	0	Sundry Debtors and Payments in						
				advance				25	2	8
Issued—3033 Shares fully paid ..	3033	0	0	Stores, Tools and Materials on hand				439	12	3
Mortgage on Freehold Property ...	400	0	0	Rolling Stock as at 30th Nov., 1917	996	6	4			
Sundry Creditors...	10	1	10	Less amount received for sale of						
				Vehicle and for damage from						
				Insurance Company ...	680	0	0			
					316	6	4			
				Less loss on sale	148	15	11			
					167	10	5			
				Additions to date	80	0	0			
								247	10	5
				Freehold Property as at 30th Nov.,						
				1917				703	5	8
				Office Furniture, Machinery, Fittings						
				as at 30th Nov., 1917 ...	182	14	6			
				Additions to date	68	12	6			
					251	7	0			
				Less Depreciation and Sales ...	37	15	6			
								213	11	6
				Gas Installation as at 30th Nov., 1917	118	18	0			
				Less amount received from Insurance						
				Company for damage... ...	22	10	0			
								96	8	0
				Revenue Account Balance at Debit						
				at 30th Nov., 1917	884	3	10			
				Add Loss for year to date... ...	805	16	3			
					1690	0	1			
				Less amount transferred from Reserve	184	0	0			
								1506	0	1
	£3443	1	10					£3443	1	10

A. E. CLARKE, *Secretary.*

THOMAS W. BAILEY,
ARTHUR E. ARMSTRONG, } *Directors.*

AUDITORS' CERTIFICATE AND REPORT TO THE SHAREHOLDERS.

We have audited the above Balance Sheet dated 30th November, 1918. We have obtained all the information and explanations we have required. In our opinion such Balance Sheet is properly drawn up so as to exhibit a true and correct view of the state of the Company's affairs, according to the best of our information and the explanations given us and as shewn in the Books of the Company.

20, BAXTER GATE, LOUGHBOROUGH,
18th December, 1918.

HERBERT GODKIN & Co.,
Auditors.

The bad news. Copy of the accounts to 30th November 1918, as a result of which it was decided to discontinue the company's activities

CONCLUSION

On 6th February 1919 an extraordinary general meeting was held at the Town Hall at which the special resolution "that the company be wound up voluntarily" was discussed and confirmed. Herbert Godkin of the company's auditors was appointed as liquidator and he took over the running of the concern with immediate effect. A meeting of creditors was advertised for 24th February, although a footnote indicated that this was to comply with the Companies Acts and that anyone with a claim against the old company should contact the liquidator promptly.

Mr Godkin discharged his duties very efficiently and a full statement of the accounts was maintained during the period of his control. This and other legal documents were eventually lodged at Companies House and provide a fascinating insight into the last few weeks of operation. The exact date of the takeover by Trent Motor Traction has always been the subject of speculation; the *Herald* in its edition of 20th February reported that the Road Car Company directors had accepted the Trent offer and that the effective date was Saturday 15th February. When the Sanitary Committee met on 19th February the Town Clerk informed the meeting that Trent would take over the business on Thursday 20th February, for which it would need four omnibus licences. It was recommended that these be granted.

Examination of the liquidators accounts reveals that car receipts, that is bus fares, totalling £15 5s. 9d. were paid in on 10th February and 15th February and that wages were paid out on 8th February and 14th February, just over £8 on each occasion. Trent paid £1517 11s. 9d. for the "sale of the company as a going concern, including all buildings and assets" on 19th February. Of this sum £430 was for the rolling stock, in fact one bus, and in addition Trent took on the responsibility for the £400 mortgage on the garage premises. It seems that the last day of Road Car operation was Saturday 15th February and the first day of Trent operation was

Thursday 20th February; with only one bus, Road Car services were restricted to certain days only.

A number of creditors presented their accounts for payment, including Loughborough Corporation for the hire of the Town Hall, 10s 6d, and for the supply of gas to the value of £20 12s. 7d., thus indicating that the bus was still running on town gas rather than petrol.   Messrs Tilling-Stevens claimed £3 2s. 4d. for spares and a rent of £5 was paid to Lloyds Bank for the use of the office in the Chambers until 25th March.   The final meeting of shareholders, to wind up the company, took place on 30th April 1919, at which Mr Godkin revealed that after legal and other expenses £1478 11s. 9d. remained to be distributed to the contributors.   A few days later Herbert Godkin signed the final papers and posted them to London, the final act after eight years of trading.   All of this activity went unrecorded in the local papers.

At the annual inspection of hackney carriages, which included buses, on 16th March 1919, Trent presented only two vehicles, not the four that had been promised.   It was not until 1920 that four vehicles were in use in Loughborough, by which time new routes had started to Derby and to Nottingham, contrary to the promise not to draw people away from the town.   In 1921 the former Road Car service to Shepshed operated on Sundays, Mondays, Thursdays and Saturdays whilst the Mountsorrel route was served every day except Friday but the frequency of both was well below that provided in the heyday of the old company.   Loughborough took its licensing powers seriously and had been inspecting vehicles for public use annually in March since 1907.   In 1923 the Omnibus Sub-committee of the Health Committee recommended that in future licences would only be granted to proprietors who met the Council's conditions on matters of vehicle safety, route, timetable and stopping places.   The Sanitary Inspector Mr Harold Bintcliffe found himself responsible for implementing these decisions whilst the committee and sub-committees invariably included men who had been involved with the Road Car Company, especially Messrs Armstrong and Bailey, their experience was not wasted!

Trent did not operate the remaining Road Car bus, which was the original Tilling-Stevens of 1912, AY 2224, but sold it for further service to the Stirling and Bridge of Allan Tramway Company in

Scotland. The sale price of £800 seems very high for an old and worn-out vehicle and in due course Trent had to refund £100 on account of the condition of the vehicle!

The former Road Car Company garage in The Rushes could accommodate six vehicles and had open parking at the rear for three more and it is evident that Trent saw an opportunity to expand its area of operations from the new Loughborough base. The company's aspirations were restricted by operating area agreements with other subsidiary companies in the BET group which established Loughborough as the southern boundary of future Trent services. New vehicles were also difficult to obtain. Trent received only one in 1918, three more in April 1919 and a further eight during the year bringing the fleet strength to twenty-six. All were Tilling-Stevens petrol-electric vehicles.

A large number of other operators established themselves in the early 1920's; in 1921 15 omnibus licences were issued for Loughborough, this had risen to 78 in 1923 and 128 in 1924. Many familiar names date from this period, including Allen, Barton, Boyer, Haywood, Horspool, Howlett, Kemp & Shaw and Potter. Most proved very tenacious and resistant to offers to purchase their businesses.

Trent maintained its Loughborough garage and operations until January 1989 when, after a period of intense competition they withdrew in favour of the Loughborough Coach and Bus Co. Ltd. This concern was a subsidiary of Leicester Citybus Ltd and Trent acquired a 6%. interest in Citybus as part of the deal. The Loughborough company was itself sold in June 1989 to Midland Fox Ltd, successors in the East Midlands to Midland Red. A few weeks later, on 22nd July, The Rushes garage housed its last buses after more than seventy-six years. Shortly afterwards the property was demolished and the site used to extend the car park of the adjacent Sainsbury's supermarket; one more link with the Loughborough Road Car Company had been severed.

Thus a chapter of Loughborough history is closed, a chapter which at the outset it was thought impossible to write due to the paucity of information. Experience has proved that in this instance a wealth of historical detail was awaiting discovery; the secret was knowing where to look and what to ask.

127652 / *25*

ᔕᗰ

THE COMPANIES ACTS, 1908 to 1917

SPECIAL RESOLUTION (pursuant to the Companies (Consolidation) Act, 1908, s. 69) of

The Loughborough Road Car Co., Ltd.

PASSED THE 13TH JANUARY, 1919.
CONFIRMED THE 6TH FEBRUARY, 1919.

REGISTERED
18381
13 FEB 1919

At Extraordinary General Meetings of the above-named Company, duly convened and held at the Town Hall, Loughborough, on the 13th day of January and the 6th day of February, 1919, respectively, the following special resolution was duly passed and confirmed :—

"That the Company be wound up voluntarily,"

And at such last mentioned Meeting, Mr. Herbert Godkin, of 20, Baxter Gate, Loughborough, Chartered Accountant, was duly appointed Liquidator for the purpose of such winding-up.

Dated this 12th day of February, 1919.

Thomas W. Bailey

Chairman.

Witness :—

R. Sutton Clifford Smith
Solicitor
Loughborough

**Printed copy of the winding up resolution as filed
with the Companies Registration Office**

50

Vehicles Operated

Registration No.	Chassis maker	Body maker	Seating

W.A.Stevens Limited, Maidstone

D 4782   Hallford-Stevens   unknown   B22R
New October 1909, used on hire in Loughborough September to December 1910.

Loughborough Road Car Company Limited

AY 2224   Tilling-Stevens TTA2   Brush   B29F
New January 1913, sold to Trent Motor Traction February 1919.

AY 2226   Tilling-Stevens TTA2   Brush   B29F
New January 1913, written off after an accident July 1918.
Both TTA2s were rebuilt to resemble Tilling-Stevens TS3 models, probably in 1914.

AY 3240   Daimler CD   Brush   O22/21R
New April 1914, chassis to War Department September 1914 and bodywork stored.

AY 4058   Edison battery bus   Brush   B22F
New July 1915, sold to Derby Corporation Tramways May 1917.

AY 4984   McCurd D   Brush   O22/21R
New January 1916, sold to unknown buyer circa May 1918.
This vehicle carried the 1914 bodywork from AY 3240.

AY 5956   Relyante   brake/landaulette
Purchased July 1918, sold circa February 1919 to Mr Bradbury, Arnold, Nottingham.

Key

B Single-deck bus;   O Open top double decker;
F Front entrance; R Rear entrance;   22/21 upper/lower deck seating capacity.

Liveries

AY 2224, 2226, 3240 & 4058 Dark Green, Light Green and Straw.
AY 4984 Brown and Straw; AY 5956 Yellow and Green.

APPENDIX B

FIRST DAYS OF RUNNING

Copy article from the *Loughborough Echo* 10th January 1913

A Good Start.

Determined to have first hand information concerning the feeling as to the buses in the Shepshed district, one of our representatives made the journey in the afternoon, but the trip cannot be said to have been inspiring nor very instructive.

The ride to Shepshed commences better than it finishes. Sedately we glided past the seats of the Loughborough mighty as befitted our progress through that exclusive district. There is not much vitality in dinginess, but there is some satisfaction in leaving or entering Loughborough by this road. As you proceed, though, you become awake to the fact that this is really commercial England, that you are really riding in a motor bus, the very latest from the hands of the intentor and the mechanic, and then the pleasant byeways and the white high road that leads away from the towns, become mere shadows in the great utilitarian scheme and you think only of the nightmare wastes of the desecrated woodlands and the disenchanted hills. These thoughts thrust themselves upon us as we proceeded, but perhaps that is not the proper light in which to regard this commercial enterprise. One person at least had no such qualms but settled down to real enjoyment, not of the scenery but of the gentle swaying motion of the bus. Should this be looked upon in the light of a testification to their easy going? Perhaps not; the person in question was at the dance with the Unionist ladies the night before, which might have been the reason of his somnolence. There is no doubt, though, that the buses run with remarkable easiness and are airy and comfortable. As we forged along at a good even rate a pedestrian stopped now and again to gaze in wonder at the new vehicle, but no one cared to pull us up to do business

As we drew near unto our destination and the murk of advancing villadom hung around the small boy came into evidence, but his attitude was doubtful and sarcasm wrestled with uproarious delight in his juvenile bosom. In one or two instances there were decided manifestations of pleasure, but when we got into the town proper—a very difficult moment to fix—the superior Shepsheders were somewhat contemptuous, and blunted their wit at the expense of the new vehicles. Many times they tried to attract the driver's attention from his business by assuring him that the back wheel was revolving, and the assertion that our bus was a " motor hearse " was not calculated to give us heart. One youth whose mind evidently ran in a sporting vein, thought that they would be extra for cricket and football teams, but the tradesmen, who had been so enthusiastic at Loughborough, wore quite a different expression, and if they ever did use " a big big D " the Shepshed tradesmen are doing it now, but they are doing it to themselves.

Local Apathy.

The locals were in no hurry to make the journey back to Loughborough, and one person of the Scrooge type carefully asked the fare before risking bankruptcy, deciding in the end to walk over a mile to the station and half a mile at the other end to save a halfpenny.

Ultimately we gathered a fair party, and every detail of the buses came in for minute scrutiny on the ride. This time we had a pick up en route, and there is no doubt that the bus was a real boon to a weary old lady whom we took aboard. She had actually never heard anything of the all-absorbing motor bus scheme until that morning, and she said it was wonderful to see " trains on the road." In capital time and without the slightest mishap we made the journey back to Loughborough, and if the company wants a testimonial that return party would be quite willing to oblige, and after a hearing it is highly probable another bus would be ordered immediately.

APPENDIX C

Table of Directors

Name, private address, business, number of shares held and period of office are given for each director.

William F. Charles, Fearon House, Loughborough.
Scent Manufacturer, Zenobia Limited, Baxtergate.
100 shares, April 1912 to December 1916; Chairman April 1912 to December 1914.

Arthur E. Armstrong, 3 Victoria Street, Loughborough.
House Furnisher, 2 Market Place.
25 later 45 shares, April 1912 to April 1919; Chairman December 1914 to 1918.

Thomas W.Bailey, 98 Herrick Road, Loughborough.
Tailor and Clothier, Bailey & Simpkin, 14/15 Market Place.
25 shares, 1913 to April 1919; Chairman 1918 to April 1919.

Henry Clemerson, White House, Leicester Road, Loughborough.
House Furnisher, Market Place.
25 later 45 shares, April 1912 to December 1917, Retired.

Albert J. Pilsbury, 59 Forest Road, Loughborough.
Draper, Young, Pilsbury & Young, 36/37 High Street.
25 shares, April 1912 to April 1919.

Henry F. Young, 26 Burton Street, Loughborough.
Draper, Young, Pilsbury & Young, 36/37 High Street.
25 shares, April 1912 to December 1913, Retired.

Joseph Deakin, 66 Beacon Road, Loughborough.
Printer & Proprietor, *Loughborough Echo*, 25 Swan St.
50 later 100 shares, April 1912 to 1914, Resigned.

Walter H. Allen, 1 Frederick Street, Loughborough.
Engineer & Manager, Loughborough Corporation Electricity Department.
50 shares, April 1912 to December 1915, Resigned.

Table continued overleaf

J. Widdowson, 1 Wards End, Loughborough.

      Basket maker, 1 Wards End.

      5 shares,. December 1914 to December 1916.

G.P.Jones, 65 Forest Road, Loughborough.

      Mechanical Engineer (retired).

      50 shares, December 1915 to 1917. Deceased.

Albert Whittaker, 20 Radmoor Road, Loughborough.

      Chemist, Market Place.

      ? shares, December 1917 to April 1919.

Herbert H. Speight, Sunny Bank, Quorn.

      Clerk.

      10 later 25 shares, December 1917 to April 1919.

John Pritchard, Leicester Road, Loughborough.

      Rope and Tent maker, Swan Street.

      10 later 60 shares, July 1918 to April 1919.

APPENDIX D

Summary of the Accounts

Year end 30 November	1912	1913	1914	1915	1916	1917	1918
	£	£	£	£	£	£	£
Traffic Receipts	nil	2158	2645	2808	2489	1839	1138
Total Income	141	2184	2672	2830	2532	1895	1150
Running Costs	nil	1155	1367	1541	1599	1413	1220
Repairs & Maintenance	nil	165	278	267	345	236	151
Management Charges	nil	213	322	383	432	384	404
Written Off	nil	342	467	475	692	268	181
Total expenses	45	1875	2434	2665	3068	2301	1956
Profit/(Loss)	96	309	237	165	(536)	(406)	(806)
Dividend Paid	5%	10%	5%	nil	nil	nil	nil
Value of Rolling Stock	670	1551	1392	1967	2077	996	247

Comment

The first full year of trading produced a profit of £309, representing 10.6% of the capital employed, but due to the increased cost of repairs in 1914 the profit was only £237 (6.7%). Further increases in expenses in 1915 caused profits to fall and the return on the capital was only 4.8%. In 1916 traffic receipts fell and running costs increased to 64% of the turnover giving a loss of £536. A similar pattern was followed in 1917 and in 1918, when the company ceased to be viable. Throughout, expenses increased disproportionately and although the concern faced many real difficulties during war time its fortunes deteriorated from the moment of incorporation. Drastic changes in the method of management were needed.

Acknowledgments

Historical research depends upon the interest and co-operation of many individuals and organisations and I am grateful to all who have responded to my enquiries or who have assisted in any way with this work. These include

BBC Written Archive Centre.
Derek M Bailey
David J Bean
Alan W Brotchie
Charnwood Borough Council
City of Derby Museums and Art Gallery
John Clarke
Companies House, Cardiff
A G Doig
Alastair Douglas
Ronald A Eden
Samuel Evans
Godkin and Co, Loughborough
Kenneth Hunt
Peter Jaques
The Kithead Trust
David Kaye
Thomas W W Knowles
Kevin Lane
Leicestershire Record Office, Wigston, Leicester
Loughborough Echo, especially Mr J D Deakin
Loughborough Library - Local History Section
Roy Marshall
Alan W. Mills
Melvin Murray
A G Newman
Alan Oxley
Public Record Office, Kew
William Stothard
Chris J. Taylor.
Andrew Webster
J.R. Wingfield

To those who contributed in any way and are not mentioned above I offer my sincere apologies.